CW00859659

Published by GuyRichardson

EASY MONEY FOR WRITERS AND WANNABES

MAGGIE COBBETT

What do I know about this? Have I made millions with my pen?

Well no. Not yet, anyway. Thwarted in an early ambition to become a journalist, I took a degree in modern languages and slid reluctantly into teaching. Writing for publication started to take a back seat then and did so even more when I married and began to juggle work with motherhood. I continued to have the odd article and short story accepted and longed for the time when I'd have the luxury of being a full time writer. Actually, I'm still waiting for that, but an unusual change of career a few years ago gave me a lot more scope.

More of that later!

A big breakthrough for me came in 2006 when I won a free place at the annual Writers' Summer School in Swanwick, an August week I'd recommend to writers of any level of experience.

What I learnt there stiffened my resolution to persevere with my own writing come what may. That first year, though, overwhelmed by the choice of courses on offer and almost burnt out midway through the week, I needed a little light relief. This I found in 'Little Fishes', a one-hour workshop on filler writing led by Colin Kilpatrick - and what an eye opener it was! In one field at least, the novice writer could compete on equal terms with the old hands and see a steady stream of cheques and prizes appearing through the letter box. All it took was a little ingenuity and a keen eye on the current market.

I made copious notes that afternoon and have been building on them ever since. At Swanwick 2012, I was proud to be invited to run a workshop of my own called 'Fulfilling Fillers'. In addition, I've had an illustrated article of the same name in *Writing Magazine* and given talks to several writers' and other interested groups on the subject. Now I'm hoping that this little reference guide will bear fruit for you!

What do I mean by a 'filler'?

'Hey, Dad! You've forgotten you're bonkers!' was the cry I once thought that I heard at a breakfast buffet in Spain. What a rude child, I thought, until I saw the sachet of sugar that he was offering to his father. I promptly pocketed one myself for future exploitation.

Originally, a filler was just a device to fill up the blank space left on a page after an article and this can still be the case. Nowadays, though, it's generally taken to be a short item, sometimes only a few words and rarely more than 250, that will amuse, intrigue or inform. Those accompanied by a photograph where possible are popular with editors and generally better paid.

The following list of suggestions is by no means exhaustive, but all have worked and continue to work for me: anecdotes of all kinds, cuttings, jokes, notices and signs that don't mean quite what they say, oddly (to us) named foreign products and dishes, puzzles, quaint translations, quizzes and useful tips about anything from creating a gourmet meal on a budget to coping with head lice. I would also include readers' letters which, whilst not strictly speaking fillers, can be very lucrative.

•

Who uses fillers?

It's probably fair to say that magazines aimed largely at a female readership offer the most obvious opportunities, but retailers' shelves nowadays are overflowing with weekly and monthly publications covering just about every legal human activity. The filler writer's horizons have never been wider. From antiques to astronomy, cat breeding to computer gaming, knitting to kayaking, new technology to nostalgia and politics to patchwork, there will be something to suit everyone's taste. For special interest titles not generally to be found at a newsagent's, I recommend consulting the *Writers & Artists Yearbook* or *Willings Press Guide.*

   Willings is far too expensive for most individuals to buy – I'm talking hundreds of pounds here – but should be available to consult in the reference section of your local library. In three large volumes entitled UK, Europe and World, it lists publications that cover everything from Accounting to Zoology. Entries include a general profile and, crucially these days, a website address. Although new editions of both *W&A* and *Willings* come out annually, there will inevitably be changes during the year and it's essential to keep up with these.

Do your homework!

Regular browsing is necessary and it's impossible to overemphasize the need to keep up to date with the market. An idea may well have been sparked off by something you read in the dentist's waiting room, but requirements and contact addresses change on a regular basis. Be warned also that a certain amount of discretion will be called for. Few of us can afford to buy every magazine or newspaper that might be of interest, but your welcome in a small shop will soon wear out if you linger too long. You're much less likely to be shown the door in a supermarket or large newsagent's.

The more you understand the market, the more successful you will be. Try to picture the average reader of any publication that interests you. The advertisements it carries will often give you a fair idea of age group, background and aspirations. Look at the 'house style'. Is it staid, up market and formal or chatty, colloquial and brash? Highly technical or designed for the novice? It's a complete waste of everyone's time to submit wildly unsuitable material on spec. Editors know their readership very well and so, with a little effort, can you. Holiday snaps of 'wardrobe malfunctions' on the beach or a tourist menu offering 'shrimp and crap salad' would be unlikely to appear in *The People's Friend* or *The Lady*. By the same token, advice on the correct storage of a top hat would be inappropriate for *Pick Me Up* or *Full House*. Only the satirical and current will do for *Private Eye*, which loves to poke fun at pretentious or idiotic statements gleaned from the media in its regular 'Commentatorballs' and 'Pseuds Corner' sections. £10 a time if yours is printed!

Fitting in with the usual length of item and range of vocabulary used will enhance your chances of acceptance. We wordsmiths – and I'm as guilty as anyone of this – can easily be tempted to show off our erudition.

That's fine when writing for *The Times* or *The Lancet*, but not so good for *That's Life*. Don't say that your husband was 'crimson of countenance' when 'red in the face' will do just as well!

Another crucial thing to establish before putting pen to paper or fingers to keyboard is if the publication in question actually pays for fillers. Some regard the honour of appearing in their pages as recompense enough! (It may well be, of course, that you feel so passionately about an issue that money is the last thing on your mind. So do I, sometimes, but that's not what this little book is about.)

Newspapers tend to fall into this category, although I did once win a free weekend at a Corus hotel of my choice from the *Daily Mail*. I'd written about a family visit to Las Vegas where, desperate to convince my sons of the futility of gambling, I put a quarter ($0.25) into a slot machine and thought that the ensuing cascade of silver coins was never going to stop. The clincher was that I was strong minded enough to exchange them for notes, walk away and spend my winnings on a very good dinner for us all.

Where to begin?

To dip your toe into the water, I recommend investing in a few cheap and cheerful magazines such as *Chat*, *Love It*, *Pick Me Up*, *Real People* and *That's Life*. They cost well under £1 each, their bright covers make them very easy to spot and they're usually grouped together on the shelves. The going rate for successful submissions as I write (March 2014) ranges from £25 to £100. (To make the most of your investment, why not also have a go at the many competitions on offer or aim for the seriously big money with a 'real life' story?)

Here's an example of an everyday tip that earned me £10 from my local newspaper. It really can be this easy!

> *If you've ever been frustrated as a new householder by the sticky labels builders leave on everything, try the following: Pull off as much of the paper as you can and then spray what's left with furniture polish and allow it to soak in before removing it very easily with a scraper or razor blade. Works like a charm!*

You may not even have to leave your own four walls to come up with ideas. Many of mine have been harvested from wisdom passed down the generations. My mother's old household management and recipe books, for example, include a wealth of useful tips designed to cut both cost and effort. My late father was a great DIY enthusiast whose triumphs (and occasional disasters) are still remembered with great fondness. Wishing that he'd passed on more of his practical skills to me, I wrote a plea to his favourite magazine that fathers should teach these to their daughters as well as their sons. To my astonishment and my husband's subsequent delight, my appeal was chosen to be Letter of the Month and

I was rewarded with a top of the range electric sander.

Our family albums, with photographs dating back well into the 19th century, have also provided a rich archive to plunder for fillers as well as my more in-depth articles on family history. How about this cutie (myself, actually, so no child exploitation issues here!) in her elastic ruched waffle nylon beach wear! Ideal for *Yours*, which loves to recall 'the way we were'.

Albums that I've compiled myself include all kinds of memorabilia collected along the way. One of my favourites is an affectionate note from a gallant young Frenchman. It includes the lines:

> *'Maggie, I have to tell you how much I loved the dress you wore the afternoon we first met and the one you had later for dinner.'*

You'll soon be bursting with ideas, but don't get carried away and send in more than one at a time to the same publication. For fillers, you're much more likely to succeed if you're seen as a loyal reader looking to share your enthusiasm, rather than a grasping writer looking for a few quid. For this reason, if your e-mail signature (or headed notepaper!) includes words like 'Writer' or 'Author', it would be advisable to remove them before sending. You'll need to supply your contact details, but there's no need for a covering letter.

Practicalities

Once you get the bit between your teeth, you'll make a point of never leaving home without the wherewithal to make notes and take photographs. Who knows what you might overhear or see while out and about? I don't have state of the art equipment, just a small notebook and my camera phone. The following image was snapped by me in a local store and went on to be snapped up by *Reader's Digest*, one of my favourite markets.

Will it cost a fortune in stationery/stamps?

With postal charges at a record high and unlikely to come down, it's fortunate that most editors nowadays are happy to receive fillers by email. Digital photography has done away with the need to risk loss or damage to your precious originals. On the other hand, editors don't yet assume that all their readers have access to modern technology.

Unlike most other submissions these days, handwritten pieces with an s.a.e. for the return of photographs are sometimes still accepted, but check that this is so. Even then, always keep copies of anything important to you. With the best will in the world, there's no guarantee that material won't go astray in a busy office.

Keeping Records

Don't send the same item to more than one publication at a time. Having agreed to print your filler, any editor would quite rightly be furious to spot it elsewhere and would probably never accept anything from you again. If, on the other hand, a few months go by and you've had no response, you're quite at liberty to send it off again.

Don't be discouraged if it's failed to hit the spot the first time round. Editors receive a great many submissions and something quite similar might have appeared recently or already be in the pipeline. If your item was seasonal, ask yourself if you sent it at the wrong time of year. Everyone needs to plan ahead and, especially for monthly publications, there can be a long lead time. The end of December would be the latest that I would send in anything relating to Easter or spring cleaning and midsummer wouldn't be too soon for Bonfire Night or Christmas related tips. It's easy to slip up, though, and I keep a written record of each submission and the outcome. On the next page is an example with some imaginary data filled in. You'll notice that the Halloween anecdote has a question mark in the final column, even though it seems to have been submitted in good time. If you're lucky, you'll be notified whether or not a contribution has been accepted and even when it's likely to appear in print. On the other hand, you may hear absolutely nothing, in which case it would be wise to check out the next few issues of the publication in question. Very rarely have I spotted anything of mine for which I haven't received the adver-

Date	Publication	Item	Outcome
05.05.13	Spooky Tales	Halloween anecdote	?
26.11.13	Nostalgia Is Us	Photo of Auntie Maureen doing the Charleston	£25 shopping voucher
03.12.14	Fisherman's Companion	Joke about artificial flies	£15 paid
14.12.14	Your Life In Our Hands	Tip about preventing eye strain at the computer	£30 paid
20.12.14	Complainers' Weekly	Letter about cold calling	Letter of the week! £40 and a stationery set

tised payment or prize, but it can happen. In that case, a very politely worded enquiry should go off to the editor. Everyone's circumstances are different, but be aware that a regular new income stream may well be of interest to the tax and/or benefits authorities. In my opinion, it's better to be up front about it.

Let the ideas flow!

I'm not above tapping my family and friends for ideas, but I usually have plenty of my own and the following categories continue to work well for me. A little 'embroidery' may occasionally be involved, but everything I send in is substantially true. This is just as well, because I've occasionally received an email or phone call requesting additional information.

Observations drawn from everyday life

These can furnish many an interesting filler. Take the child I once overheard wondering whether 'still water' was expected to change into something else! It's a fact, sad but true, that an intriguing snatch of conversation from the supermarket or a bus ride can earn the writer as much or more than a lovingly crafted short story or article. (Trust me. I know!) A delivery driver friend of mine for example was once left in stitches at a note saying "You'll find the shed open down my back passage." Respect the anonymity of your sources, though, unless you're sure that they'd be happy to be featured. Putting someone else's foibles into print without permission can lead to trouble or even the risk of being sued.

You can, of course, mine your own experiences without fear or favour. For a brief period during my teens, I sported a bun (hairstyle, not bakery product), but that stopped the night I was nearly scalped in the cinema. A man in the row behind leaned forward to retrieve something he'd dropped on the floor and caught the doughnut shaped plastic ring supporting my hair do in one of his jacket buttons. As if screaming in the middle of the film weren't humiliating enough… not even a horror film… it was my first and last date with a young man I was quite sweet on at the time.

Embarrassment followed in equal measure one Christmas years later when the double buggy I was pushing caught the edge of a carefully stacked display of glass jars of Cadbury's Roses and sent the lot crashing down. However, the letter I wrote to the store's in house magazine in praise of the friendly way the matter had been handled by the manager and staff, was rewarded with a very generous gift voucher.

Cute stories about children are always popular. I'm not a grandmother yet, but memories of my own offspring's tender years have proved very useful. A couple of examples I cherish are their conviction that Ferrybridge Power Station was God's cloud factory and the way they swallowed their grandfather's reassurance that wasps were only flies in football jerseys and therefore not to be feared. These are both among the many anecdotes of mine that have appeared in *Reader's Digest*.

Looking for material for this book, I also came across a rant I sent to *Woman's Own*, complaining about rude adults who allowed children to hold doors open for them and then stalked through without a word of thanks. It may not sound like much, but day-to-day annoyances like this can be worth hard cash, as well as offering an opportunity to vent one's spleen. *The Oldie* for instance has a dedicated 'rant' slot. (It also welcomes accounts of encounters with well known people for a section called 'I Once Met'.) Here's an example of a rant of mine, which earned me £10.

> *Why don't theatres and cinemas provide litter bins or bags for each row - or at least each section of seating. On a visit to the theatre, I overheard a five-year-old expressing amazement at all the children dropping their sweet papers and ice-cream tubs on to the floor. Have theatre and cinema managers forgotten the idea that we should "Keep Britain Tidy"?*

Observations drawn from the workplace

Every job, paid or voluntary, will throw up possibilities; anecdotes, characters, triumphs and disasters that can be turned into filler material. In my own case, I'm currently fortunate to have steady work as a 'village regular' on the Yorkshire based soap *Emmerdale*, but I spent several years before that appearing as a supporting artist ('extra') in all kinds of situations. You might still catch sight of me in old episodes of *Heartbeat*, *The Royal* and *A Touch of Frost* and I've also taken part in other television dramas, a couple of rather less than memorable films and the odd commercial. (I also once steeled my nerves to appear on *The Weakest Link*, which was every bit as scary as you might imagine.)

These experiences have provided many a filler over the years. For example, when *Heartbeat* star Tricia Penrose, aka Gina Ward, wrote an article for *Yours* about her sadness at the show's cancellation, I was able to respond immediately with my own memories and regrets.

A Heartbeat away...
I was moved by what Tricia Penrose had to say about the end of Heartbeat (Yours issue 95). Like members of Tricia's family, I worked on the show as an extra, playing many different parts over the years. I particularly remember the day I was cast as an applicant for the post of housekeeper to Lord Ashfordly. Tricia, as Gina, was with us all day, testing us on the skills required for the job, while Gwen Taylor, as Peggy, tried to scupper our efforts and secure the position for herself. We had to demonstrate flower arranging, bed-making, shirt ironing, laying a fire, mixing a Yorkshire pudding, folding a napkin and choosing wine from His Lordship's cellar. Tricia may remember me as the vegetarian extra excused pheasant plucking! I was sad to hear it will not be recommissioned, and will always remember the camaraderie and good fun we had on set.
Maggie Cobbett, Ripon, North Yorkshire

£25 Star letter

Maggie's big moment as a Heartbeat extra

"My Heartbeat heartbreak"

Having appeared as a mourner at the funeral of *Emmerdale's* Tom King, I was thrilled to be told that my photograph had appeared in *TVeasy* My hopes were dashed, though, when I discovered that I'd been bisected by the stem of a flower held up by his widow Rosemary, played by Linda Thorson. However, a very tongue in cheek letter about that bore fruit. It was unfortunate that when my complimentary copy of the magazine arrived, I discovered I'd apparently been 'dissected' instead, but I've learnt over the years to accept that mistakes will happen. After all, without them to exploit, we filler writers would be much worse off, wouldn't we? At least everything on the cheque was correct!

A real TV extra!

Q I was thrilled to see my picture in *TVeasy* recently. I was one of the mourners at Tom's funeral in *Emmerdale*. Sadly, I've been dissected by Rosemary's rose – why oh why did you choose that shot?
Maggie Cobbett, Ripon, N Yorks

A We've had a look through the archives and unfortunately there are no clearer pics of you in that scene. What a shame! Here it is again for those who missed it...

Maggie as we should have seen her (inset)!

Compiled by: Simon Timblick Photos: BBC, ITV, Rex Features

submitted IPC Media and its associated companies reserve the rig

Custa

Q As a 3 excite to be a re idea whe *Lorraine*

A Yes, C Lenny the gang noisiest, will reun on ITV1 t pies will

Handy hints

These are readily received, those with a photograph generally attracting a higher rate of pay. Simple and obvious though some tips may seem, they will always be new to someone and can refer to beauty, child care, cleaning, cookery, decorating, DIY, health, gardening, handicrafts, hobbies, pets and slimming, to name but a few. If they suggest a good way of economising on essentials, then so much the better. Many of my favourites have been passed down the family by generations of Yorkshire housewives well practised in stretching every penny as they kept their families warmly clothed, well fed and nit free. *Best* rewarded me handsomely for my advice on that particularly ticklish problem!

Reader2Reader

EARN £30!

We want your tips! Help best readers solve their health problems. Here, two readers suggest different ways to cope with head lice...

Q My children keep getting nits. What can I do to prevent them?
Sheila Holmes, Newcastle

TIP 1 Over-the-counter and prescription drugs to treat head lice aren't always effective because head lice have become resistant. Try olive oil to smother the lice and a metal nit comb.
Wendy Alstridge, Merseyside

TIP 2 Wash your children's hair in a mixture of baby shampoo and tea tree oil. It's a preventative – since I've done this we haven't had a single infestation.
Maggie Cobbett, Ripon, North Yorkshire

Maggie washes her children's hair in baby shampoo and tea tree oil

Next, readers need tips on cracked skin on heels. CAN YOU HELP? Send any tips or problems you have to: best Health, 33 Broadwick Street, London W1F 0DQ or e-mail best's health editor at *lisa.buckingham@natmags.co.uk* and include your phone number and a photo. You'll receive £30 if we publish your tip.

As another example, salsa is a passion of mine, but dance shoes can chafe and plasters don't look very elegant. (This is particularly true of the blue ones generously handed out by staff at venues where food is on offer. They clash with most of my outfits too!) Coating the top surface of my toes with petroleum jelly, however, allows me to stay on the floor for hours - and the fee I earned for this tip would cover a lifetime's supply! Find a solution to whatever frustrates you in your own life, and you can be sure that other people will be grateful for it too. Here are just three examples - I'm sure you can think of many more.

Gardening:

> *To prevent the chains of your new hanging baskets going rusty, apply a coat of clear varnish before you hang them up.*

Household:

> *Finding candles expensive? Placed in your freezer for an hour before using, they burn more slowly and evenly and drip less. Increase the light in the room by placing them in front of a mirror.*

Christmas:

> *Sick of spending hours disentangling your tree lights? Next time you take them down, wind them round a cardboard tube or a rolled up newspaper and secure the ends with sticky tape.*

Readers' letters

Some publications receive a great many letters and others hardly any. I've even heard (from a very reliable source that I don't have permission to quote) of one desperate editor asking his own staff to pen a few.

The titles mentioned below are likely to be in the first category, but it's certainly worth scanning the pages of *Willings Press Guide* for less well known ones, particularly if you have specialist knowledge that might be appreciated by, for example, the hundreds of trade and professional magazines out there.

Some editors reward the writers of every published letter. Others only choose one per issue, the payment for which can be quite substantial. *Saga* has long offered to reward up to three letters a month with £50. Other publications may send you vouchers to be spent in a high street store or garden centre or other prizes ranging from a gorgeous bouquet of flowers to a blood pressure monitor.

Friends reunited **STAR LETTER** **£100**

Without the internet the five of us girls in this photo below would never have met up again this summer.

We all used to live in the same street in Leeds and played together when we were small children. But our lives took very different paths and, until this day, we hadn't all been together for 50 years. As you can imagine, we found plenty to talk about and certainly won't lose touch again. I'm second from the left.

Maggie Cobbett, Ripon, North Yorkshire

All together now

Mint idea

My son moaned about having spots, so I told him to put toothpaste on them.

When he walked back

Specialist magazines like to make their prizes appropriate, so an appeal to experts at *Amateur Gardening* or *Gardeners' World* to tell you why your oleanders (like mine!) are refusing to flower, ingenious tip or account of an interesting visit might result in a useful clutch of National Garden vouchers. *The Horse*, on the other hand, may continue to offer vouchers for Equestrian Clearance which, I've discovered, isn't a way of disposing of riders, but rather of supplying all the tackle they might need! Many of the preparatory notes for this book were written with a handsome pen sent to me by *The Weekly News*, and the caddy of tea that arrived recently courtesy of *The People's Friend* has also helped to keep my creative juices flowing! Any rewards superfluous to your own requirements will always find a home elsewhere- relatives, friends, charities, eBay?

Successful letters often refer back to an item that's appeared in a previous issue. You might comment on an article, for example, whether you agreed with the views expressed or not. It may have inspired you or recalled an experience of your own. I once responded to a hostage story in *Reader's Digest* with an account of the time I found myself locked in a toilet in a remote part of Morocco. (This may sound frivolous, but all kinds of thoughts floated through my head during the fifteen or so minutes that passed until I was released and I was really frightened.)

On a lighter note, an article by Lynne Truss about her boyfriend's passion for photography once struck a chord with me, as my husband is similarly enthusiastic. An extract from my letter to *Woman's Journal* read:

Anyone looking at our holiday photographs would assume that I'm a single parent, as our sons and I appear on our own in almost every picture. I should have seen the warning signs at our wedding when my bridegroom and his best man nearly came to blows over possession of the camera. Fortunately, we managed to convince my new husband that it might be a good idea for him to be featured in at least some of the photographs.

It's quite rare for me to get through any publication without finding something to inspire me. This includes the free magazines offered by many retail chains. The following example was in response to a feature in Superdrug's *Spirit* magazine, and I was delighted to receive a very useful goody bag of beauty products.

Golden delicious - Your feature on fake tanning, Gold (July/ August) came at exactly the right time for me. I am going to Florida for a late summer holiday and I was dreading the prospect of being the only pallid person on the beach. Now I'll be able to step off the plane looking the part.

Sometimes an editor will even ask readers to contribute to a particular feature and I'm always happy to oblige. This was in response to an appeal from *Prima* for suggestions on how to trim the budget at Christmas time.

When wrapping presents, use string rather than tape and don't write on the paper. It can then be reused the following year.

My advice to readers of *Slimming* on how to lose weight in time for the summer was aimed at saving them pounds in both senses of the word!

Trick for the flicks - Arrive at the cinema just in time for the main picture, too late to visit the concessions stands. Drive round the block several times or even invent problems in finding a parking space, if you have to. Fortunately, no one in my family

likes to miss the beginning of a film or go out part way through,
so we save thousands of calories over the course of the year!'

The *Radio Times* offers good prizes for Letter of the Week. In a recent issue, for example, it was a DAB digital and FM radio that retails for £149.

Magazines these days often include a free gift that can be put to use. I once bought a copy of *Red* on my way through Leeds/Bradford airport, mainly to get my hands on the umbrella inside the packaging. It proved very useful in drizzly Paris and the grateful letter I wrote on my return earned me £10 to put towards another rainy day! The lipsticks, nail varnish, make up bags, hair products, flip flops etc. harvested from other magazines have proved to be excellent stocking fillers and/or tombola prizes and I've written about those too.

Travel

You might begin with places in your own area that would interest visitors. Unusual architecture, specialist shops and quaint local customs are only three of many avenues that you could explore. My adopted city of Ripon is awash with them, from the 7th century crypt in the Cathedral to the nightly setting of the watch by our much loved Hornblower. The following anecdote appeared in *Woman's Weekly*:

It all adds up - On holiday in China my husband and I were surprised to see the abacus still widely used in department stores as well as in small shops. The only electronic calculator we saw was in Beijing (Peking) airport when we went to have our currency changed at the end of our stay. The young clerk deftly calculated how much money we were due and then took it to his senior to be checked - with an abacus!

When further afield, I also take the opportunity to send in a few lines and a photograph about my experiences, good or bad. (If bad, be sure that you can prove what you write! Nobody objects to praise.) Always be prepared! *Pick Me Up* stipulated that I should include a photograph of myself in situ with my favourite holiday reading – said magazine, of course –and I was very happy to oblige!

It's often been said that the UK and the USA are separated by a common language and examples aren't hard to find. How about this sign I spotted in Florida?

'Custodial' marked a sinister looking door in Universal Studios. A place of confinement for unruly holidaymakers? Not so. It was just a store for cleaning equipment, 'custodians' being the maintenance team. That said, don't rush to photograph pictures of things proudly displaying the word 'pants', or demand to know if people actually rest in the restroom. Decades of American television have well and truly taken the humour out of that kind of usage. However, a 'fanny-pack' instead of 'bum-bag' can still raise a laugh, and it's only here in the UK that you'll find rubbers sold at stationery counters instead of pharmacies! Photo opportunities for everyone abound in the great American theme parks. Yes, it is one of my own sons with the circle round his head on Page 29. We shared the £50!

British travellers Down Under may still be surprised to find thongs in the shoe department rather than with the lingerie. On another note, as a lover of the bright red flowers we see in our cornfields, this sign from Tasmania gave me quite a start.

Sometimes readers are asked to send in details of their favourite holiday spots, at home or abroad. This one of mine appeared in *Woman's Weekly*.

Boldly going Trekking

Quick, beam him up, Scottie!
Here's my son, David,
posing for a photo onboard
the Enterprise on a recent trip
to Las Vegas in America. We're
all very proud of him, and we're
sure he'll be able to help the rest
of the crew beat off those
dreaded Klingons.
Maggie Cobbett
North Yorkshire

£5

YO

Send us y
it, we'll se
with your
photo, or
can't retu
you'll get
Up, Come
King's Rea
Street, Lo
forget to i
age, addr
number. '
us throug

Photographs

My camera phone accompanies me everywhere and I delight in capturing odd situations and ambiguous signs, especially those 'professionally' produced. Misplaced apostrophes on their own are not normally sufficient. Look for signs that go out of their way to make you cringe. Like this one:

When a branch of Booths supermarket opened in my North Yorkshire city of Ripon, I was amused to see that its stock of Lancashire Tea remained untouched whilst all the Yorkshire Tea flew off the shelf. I took a photograph, and sold it to *Reader's Digest* with a quip about the Wars of the Roses. In the same store, I found this loaf of bread crying out for help.

'Curiously' shaped 'vegetables have been popular with the public since the 1970s, when Esther Rantzen first featured them in her television programme *That's Life*, so why not bakery products as well? Someone behind the scenes must have been having a bad day when I spotted some iced doughnuts with really miserable faces. Unfortunately, I'd neglected to recharge my phone that day and they'd disappeared by the time I got back to the store. Lesson learnt! Another one I missed was a pub advertising "GREAT FOOD EXCEPT ON TUESDAYS". By the time I returned, someone had apparently told the manager. Curses!

An unexpected 'hit' was a shot of a curious sign in the foyer of our local swimming pool. It told customers that, due to essential maintenance work, all females should use the male changing room and all males the female one. I never did find out how that was supposed to ease the situation, but the cheque from *Reader's Digest* eased mine.

I've already mentioned my family albums. They've made many a contribution to 'nostalgia' pages, from a photo of an uncle who married very young and survived the trenches of World War 1 to a hippy wedding ceremony. Look out for photographs that lend themselves to a variety of themes. The uncle here, for example, although wounded by a piece of shrapnel and left with the full use of only one arm, went on to run a chicken farm and then to be gardener to a well known actor. And just look at those hats worn by his bride and her sister!

It's very important, of course, to be sensitive to the feelings of descendants, particularly if the photograph is unflattering. As I've already pointed out, using shots of people still alive without their permission can also lead to trouble and, most important of all, never ever submit a photograph of an identifiable child, even a family member, without first obtaining the consent of the parents.

Images of yourself, of course, flattering or otherwise, are absolutely fine. This winsome teenager in a new dress and with her first proper boyfriend appeared in *Yours*! Yes, once again, it's yours truly.

We're a nation of animal lovers and your pets, large or small, can help to pay for their keep. My own cats are blissfully unaware of the contributions they've made over the years. You might write about how they came to live with you, the names you chose for them, difficulties settling them in, how they react to family members and other pets, food preferences, quirks of behaviour… the possibilities are endless.

A cat standing on its hind legs begging for food has more appeal than one coughing up a hairball or disembowelling a mouse! Of course, it doesn't have to be doing something *conventionally* cute to be funny.

The animal need not belong to you, of course. Other proud owners may be flattered by requests to capture their own pets' winning ways, particularly if you share the proceeds with them. The countryside, zoos and safari parks should also give you plenty of scope for cute, amusing or unusual shots. A beady eyed goat hovering around your picnic lunch might provide a winning animal 'selfie'.

PLEASE DON'T FEED FINGERS TO THE ANIMALS

Zoos especially often have a great range of warning signs, sometimes funny in themselves but particularly when ignored at the visitor's peril and you can capture the moment. Splash Zones around the habitats of aquatic animals are good for this and, even more so, the 'Splatter Zone' around others. If a rhinoceros defiantly turns its back on a visitor, the ensuing spray can be both messy and pungent!

Safari parks allow you to get even closer to some animals, which may or may not be a good thing. How about a photo of monkeys at Longleat attacking your windscreen wipers? Well, maybe not, but a shot of a zebra crossing might appeal to an editor who enjoys puns!

Cuttings

It's well worth keeping a pair of scissors and a highlighter pen to hand when you sit down to read a newspaper, magazine or even an advertising leaflet. It won't be long before you find the odd howler. One of my favourite clippings is of a fitted kitchen that boasts a '300 mm Pullout Panty.' Other gems have included a stately home which apparently once had 'canons' to defend it, a canal side house with attractive 'toe path' walks on its doorstep and the police discovery of a stolen 'horde' in a deserted farmhouse. Militant clerics, ballerinas *en pointe* and the final resting place of Genghis Khan's armies all faithfully reported!

In other examples, an unfortunate impression may be given even when there is nothing actually wrong with the text. The following advert leapt out at me from the entertainment section of our local paper, and how I pitied the losing porkers!

Pig racing at the New Inn, 8PM. Bacon butties from 9PM

Or how about this wedding announcement?

The bride is a police officer in West Yorkshire and the bride-groom a Platoon Sergeant 1st Battalion Yorkshire Regiment, Germany. The bride's interests are hockey/gym and the bride-groom's fitness.

Enough said! Both these fine examples have appeared in *Reader's Digest*.

Jokes

Those you submit can be simple or complex, family friendly, slightly risqué or very near the knuckle, depending on the target publication *That's Life* actually invites readers to send in entries for 'John's Rude Joke Of The Week'. (For the sake of marital harmony, I would never contribute to the 'Aren't Men Daft?' slot on the same page, although you might!) It's often said that there is no such thing as a new joke but, like the helpful tips I mentioned earlier, it will always be new to someone. Take this one of mine, for example, which appeared in *Reader's Digest*.

I saw a collision between a red lorry and a yellow lorry. The police asked me who was to blame. I said it was hard to say

Did that make you groan? Well, maybe, but it earned me a useful cheque.

John's RUDE JOKE of the week

'You know that girl who lives next door to us?' Adam says to his flatmate. 'I wish she'd get her boyfriend to move in with her.'
'Why?' his flatmate asks.
'Well,' Adam explains, 'she's always having phone sex with him till the early hours, with the speaker on, and it keeps me awake. At least if they live together, it'll be over in five minutes and I'll get some sleep.'

Make me laugh - send me your rude jokes!

Puzzles and Quizzes

Have you ever wondered who invents the brainteasers in your favourite publications? If you have a bright idea, why not submit it for the editor's consideration? *Chat* for example offers £20 for a 4x4 crossword submitted by a reader and *Real People* has a whole page of Reader Puzzles with £30 paid for each one published and £50 for the Puzzler Of The Week. Time to get the thinking cap on! (Or cheat, and download some puzzle making software from the internet.) This kind of item may be, but isn't necessarily, seasonal. Without being patronising, you should aim for a degree of difficulty suitable for the average reader of the publication targeted.

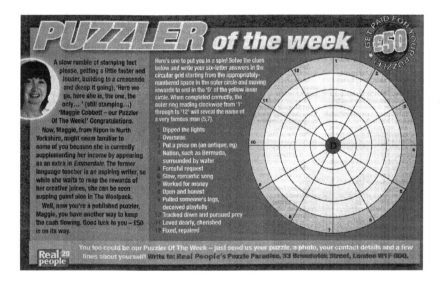

References

The publications mentioned in this book are listed here in alphabetical order, but don't forget that there are many more out there for you to investigate. Editors (and titles) come and go and requirements change all the time, so it's over to you now to keep your finger on the pulse!

Amateur Gardening	That's Life
Best	The Horse
Chat	The Lady
Daily Mail	The Lancet
Full House	The Oldie
Gardeners' World	The People's Friend
Love It	The Times
Pick Me Up	The Weekly News
Prima	TVeasy
Private Eye	Willings Press Guide
Reader's Digest	Woman's Journal
Real People	Woman's Own
Red	Woman's Weekly
Saga	Writing Magazine
Slimming	Writers' & Artists' Yearbook
Spirit	Yours

Final Thoughts

In conclusion, I'd like to thank you for investing in this book. If you follow my suggestions, you'll get your money back many times over. Feel free to contact me via my website www.maggiecobbett.co.uk with any questions or comments you may have.

I'd particularly like to hear about your successes!

About The Author

Born in Leeds, Maggie Cobbett ventured across the Pennines to study at the University of Manchester and then spent more years than she cares to remember teaching French, German and EFL in the UK and abroad. Now settled with her family and two ex-feral cats on the edge of the Yorkshire Dales, Maggie takes inspiration for her writing from her surroundings, travels, family history and her work as a television background artist.

OTHER BOOKS BY MAGGIE COBBETT

ANYONE FOR MURDER?
A selection of murder mysteries to keep you
guessing until the very end.

HAD WE BUT WORLD ENOUGH
Life in a new country sounds enticing, but will the hopeful
characters in these short stories end up with more or much,
much less than they bargained for?

SWINGS & ROUNDABOUTS
In fiction as in life, things rarely turn out as we expect.
Plenty of surprises await characters and readers alike in
this third collection of short stories.

ALL TITLES AVAILABLE ON AMAZON, ON
KINDLE, AND IN A PRINT OMNIBUS

WWW.MAGGIECOBBETT.CO.UK

Printed in Great Britain
by Amazon.co.uk, Ltd.,
Marston Gate.